Vision

Board

Journal

"Write it, See it, Believe it"

Venita Alderman

Vision Board Journal
Copyright ©2018 by Venita Alderman

ISBN: 978-1981981939

4-5 Essentials
PO Box 1782
Wake Forest NC 27588

Cover design and images by Rebecca Pau @
The Final Wrap.

For more information on Venita visit
www.VenitaAlderman.com

The Vision Board Journal is a reference for all the things you put on your vision board and/or for things you wish to just accomplish.

My hope is that this helps you stay on target and guide you to the success you wish to attain.

This journal can be used at any time of the year. You will write it (your vision) down, look at it (your vision) daily and/or weekly and believe these things (your vision) will become reality.

YOU must work toward your vision, it can be done. Focus, stay on track and remain positive.

~Enjoy your journey~

Vision without action is merely a dream;
Action without vision just passes the time;
Vision with action can change the world.
~Joel A Barker

What is your Vision/Vision Board Name?

_____

Why did you pick the name?

_____

_____

_____

_____

The Just Live by Faith

[2] Then the LORD answered me and said:

"Write the vision
And make *it* plain on tablets,
That he may run who reads it

Habakkuk 2:2

What do you envision for the next 30 Days?

_____

_____

_____

_____

_____

_____

60 Day Vision?

_____

_____

_____

_____

_____

_____

90 Day Vision?

_____

_____

_____

_____

_____

180 Day Vision?

_____

_____

_____

_____

_____

_____

1-year Vision?

_____

_____

_____

_____

_____

_____

_____

_____

_____

_____

_____

_____

_____

Goals

Categories

(you can fill in/make changes)

Faith/Spirituality

_____

_____

Therefore, I say to you, whatever things you ask when you pray, believe that you receive *them,* and you will have *them.*

Mark 11:24

Faith is knowing things will get better, even though; you can't see, hear or feel it. ~va

Why do I have this goal?

_____

_____

_____

_____

_____

What is my timeline for this goal?

_____

_____

_____

_____

_____

What steps do I need to take to fulfil this goal?

_____

_____

_____

_____

_____

What obstacles do I need to overcome to fulfil this goal?

_____

_____

_____

_____

_____

Is this goal for me or someone else?

_____

_____

_____

_____

_____

When I complete this goal, I will feel:

_____

_____

_____

_____

_____

Health/Fitness/Meals

_____

_____

Beloved, I pray that you may prosper in all things and be in health, just as your soul prospers.

3 John 1:2

Being healthy starts from the inside. Go have a conversation with your doctor and start making the necessary changes, one step (walking/jogging) at a time, one meal (portions/changes) at a time. ~va

Why do I have this goal?

_____

_____

_____

_____

_____

What is my timeline for this goal?

_____

_____

_____

_____

_____

What steps do I need to take to fulfil this goal?

_____

_____

_____

_____

_____

What obstacles do I need to overcome to fulfil this goal?

_____

_____

_____

_____

_____

Is this goal for me or someone else?

_____

_____

_____

_____

_____

When I complete this goal, I will feel:

_____

_____

_____

_____

_____

Career/Entrepreneurship

_____

_____

Then he who had received the one talent came and said, 'Lord, I knew you to be a hard man, reaping where you have not sown, and gathering where you have not scattered seed.

Matthew 25:24

Passion is what separates you from having a career you love or just working a 9-5 job. ~va

Why do I have this goal?

_____

_____

_____

_____

_____

What is my timeline for this goal?

_____

_____

_____

_____

_____

What steps do I need to take to fulfil this goal?

_____

_____

_____

_____

_____

What obstacles do I need to overcome to fulfil this goal?

_____

_____

_____

_____

_____

Is this goal for me or someone else?

_____

_____

_____

_____

_____

When I complete this goal, I will feel:

_____

_____

_____

_____

_____

Self-Improvement/Reputation

But the LORD said to Samuel, "Do not look at his appearance or at his physical stature, because I have refused him. For *the LORD does not see* as man sees; for man looks at the outward appearance, but the LORD looks at the heart.

1 Samuel 16:7

The only competition you should have is the person staring you back in the mirror. Go look, then work on the discrepancies. ~va

Why do I have this goal?

_____

_____

_____

_____

_____

What is my timeline for this goal?

_____

_____

_____

_____

_____

What steps do I need to take to fulfil this goal?

_____

_____

_____

_____

_____

What obstacles do I need to overcome to fulfil this goal?

_____

_____

_____

_____

_____

Is this goal for me or someone else?

_____

_____

_____

_____

_____

When I complete this goal, I will feel:

_____

_____

_____

_____

_____

Family

_____

_____

But if anyone does not provide for his own,
and especially for those of his household, he
has denied the faith and is worse than an
unbeliever.

1 Timothy 5:8

Family is the people I love, cherish and want
to make/have memories with. ~va

Why do I have this goal?

_____

_____

_____

_____

_____

What is my timeline for this goal?

_____

_____

_____

_____

_____

What steps do I need to take to fulfil this goal?

_____

_____

_____

_____

_____

What obstacles do I need to overcome to fulfil this goal?

_____

_____

_____

_____

_____

Is this goal for me or someone else?

_____

_____

_____

_____

_____

When I complete this goal, I will feel:

_____

_____

_____

_____

_____

Finances/Prosperity

_____

_____

Give, and it will be given to you: good
measure, pressed down, shaken together, and
running over will be put into your bosom. For
with the same measure that you use, it will be
measured back to you.

Luke 6:38

I'm happy to receive my paycheck biweekly,
but I'll be extremely happy when I am not
living by it. Financial freedom is the goal. ~va

Why do I have this goal?

_____

_____

_____

_____

_____

What is my timeline for this goal?

_____

_____

_____

_____

_____

What steps do I need to take to fulfil this goal?

_____

_____

_____

_____

_____

What obstacles do I need to overcome to fulfil this goal?

_____

_____

_____

_____

_____

Is this goal for me or someone else?

_____

_____

_____

_____

_____

When I complete this goal, I will feel:

_____

_____

_____

_____

_____

Friends

_____

_____

Most men will proclaim each his own
goodness,
But who can find a faithful man?

Proverbs 20:6

A friend is someone that is *there* for you;
through the good, bad and horrible times.
Them being there through the laughter and
the tears. ~va

Why do I have this goal?

_____

_____

_____

_____

_____

What is my timeline for this goal?

_____

_____

_____

_____

_____

What steps do I need to take to fulfil this goal?

_____

_____

_____

_____

_____

What obstacles do I need to overcome to fulfil
this goal?

_____

_____

_____

_____

_____

Is this goal for me or someone else?

_____

_____

_____

_____

_____

When I complete this goal, I will feel:

_____

_____

_____

_____

_____

Education

_____

_____

For wisdom *is* a defense *as* money *is* a
defense,
But the excellence of knowledge *is that*
wisdom gives life to those who have it.

Ecclesiastes 7:12

Once you learn something, it's never
forgotten. Learn something new daily. ~va

Why do I have this goal?

_____

_____

_____

_____

_____

What is my timeline for this goal?

_____

_____

_____

_____

_____

What steps do I need to take to fulfil this goal?

_____

_____

_____

_____

_____

What obstacles do I need to overcome to fulfil this goal?

_____

_____

_____

_____

_____

Is this goal for me or someone else?

_____

_____

_____

_____

_____

When I complete this goal, I will feel:

_____

_____

_____

_____

_____

Love/Relationships

_____

_____

His left hand *is* under my head,
And his right hand embraces me.

Song of Solomon 8:3

Love is a verb, a verb is action, action is
movement. Show it daily. ~va

Why do I have this goal?

_____

_____

_____

_____

_____

What is my timeline for this goal?

_____

_____

_____

_____

_____

What steps do I need to take to fulfil this goal?

_____

_____

_____

_____

_____

What obstacles do I need to overcome to fulfil this goal?

_____

_____

_____

_____

_____

Is this goal for me or someone else?

_____

_____

_____

_____

_____

When I complete this goal, I will feel:

_____

_____

_____

_____

_____

Travel/Vacations

_____

_____

But that the world may know that I love the Father, and as the Father gave Me commandment, so I do. Arise, let us go from here.

John 14:31

There is nothing wrong with physically going to a different country, island, etc. I personally enjoy a good book, that's my escape. ~va

Why do I have this goal?

_____

_____

_____

_____

_____

What is my timeline for this goal?

_____

_____

_____

_____

_____

What steps do I need to take to fulfil this goal?

_____

_____

_____

_____

_____

What obstacles do I need to overcome to fulfil this goal?

_____

_____

_____

_____

_____

Is this goal for me or someone else?

_____

_____

_____

_____

_____

When I complete this goal, I will feel:

_____

_____

_____

_____

_____

Other

_____

_____

Why do I have this goal?

_____

_____

_____

_____

_____

What is my timeline for this goal?

_____

_____

_____

_____

_____

What steps do I need to take to fulfil this goal?

_____

_____

_____

_____

_____

What obstacles do I need to overcome to fulfil this goal?

_____

_____

_____

_____

_____

Is this goal for me or someone else?

_____

_____

_____

_____

_____

When I complete this goal, I will feel:

_____

_____

_____

_____

_____

Other

_____

_____

Why do I have this goal?

_____

_____

_____

_____

What is my timeline for this goal?

_____

_____

_____

_____

What steps do I need to take to fulfil this goal?

_____

_____

_____

_____

_____

What obstacles do I need to overcome to fulfil

this goal?

_____

_____

_____

_____

_____

Is this goal for me or someone else?

_____

_____

_____

_____

_____

When I complete this goal, I will feel:

_____

_____

_____

_____

_____

Other

_____

_____

Why do I have this goal?

_____

_____

_____

_____

_____

What is my timeline for this goal?

_____

_____

_____

_____

_____

What steps do I need to take to fulfil this goal?

_____

_____

_____

_____

_____

What obstacles do I need to overcome to fulfil this goal?

_____

_____

_____

_____

_____

Is this goal for me or someone else?

_____

_____

_____

_____

_____

When I complete this goal, I will feel:

_____

_____

_____

_____

_____

Other

_____

_____

Why do I have this goal?

_____

_____

_____

_____

What is my timeline for this goal?

_____

_____

_____

_____

What steps do I need to take to fulfil this goal?

_____

_____

_____

_____

_____

What obstacles do I need to overcome to fulfil this goal?

_____

_____

_____

_____

_____

Is this goal for me or someone else?

_____

_____

_____

_____

_____

When I complete this goal, I will feel:

_____

_____

_____

_____

_____

Other

_____

_____

Why do I have this goal?

_____

_____

_____

_____

What is my timeline for this goal?

_____

_____

_____

_____

_____

What steps do I need to take to fulfil this goal?

_____

_____

_____

_____

_____

What obstacles do I need to overcome to fulfil this goal?

_____

_____

_____

_____

_____

Is this goal for me or someone else?

_____

_____

_____

_____

_____

When I complete this goal, I will feel:

_____

_____

_____

_____

_____

First
30 Days

Day 1

What have you done to work toward your goal/goals today?

_____

_____

_____

_____

_____

Day 2

What have you done to work toward your goal/goals today?

_____

_____

_____

_____

_____

_____

Day 3

What have you done to work toward your goal/goals today?

_____

_____

_____

_____

_____

_____

Day 4

What have you done to work toward your goal/goals today?

_____

_____

_____

_____

_____

_____

Day 5

What have you done to work toward your goal/goals today?

_____

_____

_____

_____

_____

Day 6

What have you done to work toward your goal/goals today?

_____

_____

_____

_____

_____

_____

Day 7

What have you done to work toward your goal/goals today?

_____

_____

_____

_____

_____

_____

Day 8

What have you done to work toward your goal/goals today?

_____

_____

_____

_____

_____

Day 9

What have you done to work toward your goal/goals today?

_____

_____

_____

_____

_____

_____

Day 10

What have you done to work toward your goal/goals today?

_____

_____

_____

_____

_____

_____

Day 11

What have you done to work toward your goal/goals today?

_____

_____

_____

_____

_____

_____

Day 12

What have you done to work toward your goal/goals today?

_____

_____

_____

_____

_____

Day 13

What have you done to work toward your goal/goals today?

_____

_____

_____

_____

_____

_____

Day 14

What have you done to work toward your goal/goals today?

_____

_____

_____

_____

_____

_____

Day 15

What have you done to work toward your goal/goals today?

_____

_____

_____

_____

_____

_____

Day 16

What have you done to work toward your goal/goals today?

_____

_____

_____

_____

_____

_____

Day 17

What have you done to work toward your
goal/goals today?

_____

_____

_____

_____

_____

_____

Day 18

What have you done to work toward your
goal/goals today?

_____

_____

_____

_____

_____

_____

Day 19

What have you done to work toward your goal/goals today?

_____

_____

_____

_____

_____

Day 20

What have you done to work toward your goal/goals today?

_____

_____

_____

_____

_____

_____

Day 21

What have you done to work toward your goal/goals today?

_____

_____

_____

_____

_____

_____

Day 22

What have you done to work toward your
goal/goals today?

_____

_____

_____

_____

_____

Day 23

What have you done to work toward your
goal/goals today?

_____

_____

_____

_____

_____

_____

Day 24

What have you done to work toward your goal/goals today?

_____

_____

_____

_____

_____

Day 25

What have you done to work toward your goal/goals today?

_____

_____

_____

_____

_____

_____

Day 26

What have you done to work toward your goal/goals today?

_____

_____

_____

_____

_____

Day 27

What have you done to work toward your goal/goals today?

_____

_____

_____

_____

_____

_____

Day 28

What have you done to work toward your
goal/goals today?

_____

_____

_____

_____

_____

Day 29

What have you done to work toward your goal/goals today?

_____

_____

_____

_____

_____

Day 30

What have you done to work toward your goal/goals today?

_____

_____

_____

_____

60 Days
thru
1-Year

60 Day

What have you accomplished toward your
goal/goals?

_____

_____

_____

_____

_____

_____

_____

_____

_____

_____

_____

What do you need to work on/what is distracting you?

_____

_____

_____

_____

_____

_____

_____

_____

_____

_____

_____

_____

_____

Additional Information

_____

_____

_____

_____

_____

_____

_____

_____

_____

_____

_____

_____

_____

_____

_____

90 Day

What have you accomplished toward your
goal/goals?

_____

_____

_____

_____

_____

_____

_____

_____

_____

_____

_____

What do you need to work on/what is distracting you?

_____

_____

_____

_____

_____

_____

_____

_____

_____

_____

_____

_____

_____

_____

Additional Information

180 Day

What have you accomplished toward your goal/goals?

_____

_____

_____

_____

_____

_____

_____

_____

_____

_____

_____

What do you need to work on/what is
distracting you?

_____

_____

_____

_____

_____

_____

_____

_____

_____

_____

_____

_____

Additional Information

_____

_____

_____

_____

_____

_____

_____

_____

_____

_____

_____

_____

_____

_____

_____

1-Year

What have you accomplished toward your goal/goals?

_____

_____

_____

_____

_____

_____

_____

_____

_____

_____

_____

_____

What do you need to work on/what is
distracting you?

_____

_____

_____

_____

_____

_____

_____

_____

_____

_____

_____

_____

_____

Additional Information

NOTES

Venita Alderman

creativity unleashed

Made in the USA
San Bernardino, CA
08 August 2019